Shadows & Reflections

Shadows & Reflections

NANCY CHISHOLM HASKETT

IF BOOKS

Modesto, California

*Design & photo collages for the six
thematic subdivisions in this book
by Mark S. Haskett.*

CONTENTS

Preface

In early 1988, I came across a short article in *The Modesto Bee*, our local newspaper, which called for submissions to a "Poets' Corner" contest, an annual writing competition I'd never heard of previously. I submitted one of my poems and some weeks later was thrilled to receive notification that I was one of its category winners, and I was now invited to read my poem at a special awards ceremony. The following year I looked again for the contest announcement, wrote a second winning poem… and I was hooked!

Despite my career as a junior high English teacher that left precious little time to write, I was determined to create at least one good poem every year for submission to the Poets' Corner, hoping to lengthen my winning streak. That "streak" turned out to be not so short, stretching from 1988 until the year of the pandemic, with one or two poems selected in each of those years.

Writing poetry was nothing new for me. I'd been writing poems ever since elementary school but had never before considered entering a citywide contest. After fifteen consecutive years of Poets' Corner winners, however, I'd developed enough confidence to enter other contests as well, and for the first time my poems appeared in several local publications. When I retired from my teaching job in 2011, I was invited to join a small group of other poets who met monthly to share and critique each other's work. These women both inspired and encouraged me to write regularly, and to send out my work for consideration in a variety of other contests and journals. I've been able to devote even more time to that effort in recent years.

(continued on next page)

Many of the poems in this collection have not only been published and won multiple awards, but more importantly are among my personal favorites, spanning the years from 1990 to 2022. Although I still enter a contest on occasion, I write primarily as a means of expressing myself, often in response to everyday events and memories from the past… my family, travels, daily walks, what's happening in the news. Many of these poems have also been strengthened by the sharp eyes and helpful suggestions of other poets in my writing groups, and I am especially grateful for my Sestina Sisters and their continued love and support.

Finally, this book would never have been published without my husband Mark, who has been encouraging me to put together a collection for many years. I have finally given him the contents, but he has done all of the work to create its finished form… a true labor of love! For that reason and more, he is the one to whom I owe the most thanks.

Nancy Haskett
June, 2022

3

Berkeley, 1969

We had come to Oakland
for the first time,
my fiancé and I,
to spend Thanksgiving weekend
with a friend in art college.
She took us to the Berkeley campus,
one of the dormitories
rising above the trees,
huge, hand-lettered signs in descending windows:
END
THE
WAR
NOW.

Later, we walked along University Avenue,
watched Hare Krishnas in their saffron robes,
girls in long skirts of multi-colored squares,
ankle bracelets that chimed as they moved barefoot
down the sidewalk, through haze of pot smoke, incense,
Abbey Road playing everywhere
from tinny transistor radios;
we wore seed bead necklaces around our necks,
watched *Easy Rider* in a crowded theater
after our turkey dinner.

On a bus back to the airport,
the only other passengers were soldiers
dressed in Army fatigues,
each one in a seat,
alone,
rows apart in the darkness.
Our final destination, Long Beach,
theirs, likely Saigon —
an almost empty bus
crowded with emotion,
our reflections ghost-like
in darkened windows.

Subdivision

A menacing presence of earthmovers,
unwelcome neighborhood invaders,
encamp at the end of our street,
their headlights piercing wintry morning fog
in glaring contrast to colorful Christmas lights
glowing softly on nearby houses.

Oddly silent, vulture-like,
they wait patiently
for our last pastoral hopes to die,
ready to dig up, carve out, uproot,
scatter and scavenge
the nearby orchard and vineyard.

Come spring,
the sound of hammers will muffle birds' cries,
rooftops replace almond trees,
cement curbs frame our weekend bike route,
no longer surrounded by showers of falling blossoms
and the symphony of bees.

Only the canal will remain,
flowing incongruously
behind new cinderblock fences
and backyard barbecues,
a quiet and constant reminder
of what is lost.

Fabrication

With the dexterity of Arachne,
politicians possess an uncanny ability
to take one thin thread of truth,
unspool all of it,
pick up a sharp needle,
create a quilt of knots and lies
with no logic or pattern,
the facts now reversed, torn, entangled,
hidden from view.

Once the fabrication is complete,
it's impossible to find
where the thread began;
even more alarming,
the end is nowhere in sight,
nothing to yank on,
to unravel it all
at the seams.

Sometimes I think about the dogs

running on roads,
desperate,
trapped in the center divide
of a Massachusetts freeway,
frantic
unable to reach the other side,
nowhere for us to pull over safely
to attempt a rescue

another just a dark blur
bolting across three lanes
to end under the wheel of our car
as we sped toward L.A. at 70 miles per hour,
too dangerous to slam on brakes

then just last week,
the one loping in the rain
along Highway 41
directly in front of us
as we rounded a curve
on the winding two-lane road

they run through
my conscience
trailing
muddy leashes of guilt.

Protest

Forever a child of the sixties,
I bought black grosgrain ribbon at the craft store,
cut off a small section and wrapped it around my left arm —
a conscious political statement against this latest war.

Most people didn't seem to notice.
A few made polite inquiries,
appeared satisfied with my answer,
often hesitant to pursue
an uncomfortable conversation.

It was meant as an outward sign,
a visible reminder to others
that some of us
still
don't quietly acquiesce.
I hadn't expected it would become something else for me...
a constant feeling of restricted movement,
a daily reminder of the reason I was wearing it,
an ever-present constriction,
like a squeezing of my heart.

Change Gonna Come

I.
Once again
streets fill with protestors
in 1960s deja vu,
marchers hold hands, raise signs,
voices unite in chants
as police hurl tear gas and pepper spray,
non-violence shatters
with store-front windows.

We have seen this before.
We have done this before.
And yet, this time it feels different,
a global outcry,
from Minneapolis to Berlin,
Los Angeles to London,
New York City to Hong Kong,
and this time,
it isn't centuries of repression
or years of an unpopular war
that light the spark;
this time it's 8 minutes and 46 seconds
of a bystander's video
to show that all we've done
isn't enough,
isn't even close to being enough,
and the time for change is now.

II.
In Missouri,
a young college graduate with insight and persistence,
convinces Merriam-Webster
to expand its definition of "racism"
because it's more than
simply personal prejudice
when the whole system is rigged,
when the oppression runs deep within society
no matter how hard you try.
Just one small change,
just one addition to an entry on a page
with all the other words,
a revision that reflects the truer reality,
makes it harder to hide behind excuses,
broadens the perspective —
one small change
that is, nevertheless,
transformational.

Ash

As I walk today
in hazy heavy air,
I pass cars, plants, mailboxes
dusted with fine gray powder,
and I breathe in
these same particles,
from wildfires all around our valley.

In camps like Treblinka, Sobibor, and Auschwitz,
the ash fell thick like snow
twenty-four hours a day,
while local citizens denied knowledge of these places,
swept dust from porches and windowsills.

The guards who worked within feet of the chimneys
inhaled fragments of their victims every day,
took in air filled with infinitesimal pieces
of men who had read from the Torah every Shabbat,
women who had baked challah and lit candles,
children who had practiced their Hebrew lessons.

With every life-giving inhalation
they breathed in those who no longer breathed,
absorbed them into their lungs, their blood,
close to their heart.

On "Landscape with the Fall of Icarus" *

Charleston, Aurora, Columbine,
Newtown, Virginia Tech,
Paris, Las Vegas —
places that roll off our tongues too easily,
a litany of violence become commonplace.
Shock worn off, once riveted to news broadcasts,
we pay less attention now
or don't look at all,
like the plowman and shepherd in the painting,
absorbed in the routine of their daily lives,
too preoccupied to notice the tragedy,
even as Icarus falls from the sky
into the blue-green waters.

**Painting usually attributed
to Pieter Bruegel*

Charles Wysocki's World

Created from his paintings,
the jigsaw puzzles
depict nostalgic Americana:
Victorian houses and street scenes,
wide lawns and stained-glass windows.
Children wave American flags,
an ice cream vendor plays hop-scotch on the sidewalk.

Beside Cape Cod homes and beaches,
fine horses pull carriages along cobblestones
to bakeries, antique shops, past white picket fences.
Men wear suspenders, bow ties and hats,
young girls hold hands and bouquets of flowers,
little boys wear breeches and smiles.

In the Wild West,
a small crowd of men and women
jabber happily on the porch of a saloon,
the gambling hall and land office inviting and innocent,
a steam train carries passengers across a trestle bridge,
a waterfall cascades in the distance.

In front of the brick police station,
seven officers stand at attention;
they wear identical uniforms, expressions,
bright, brass buttons and badges,
the sign behind them: an eagle with golden wings,
the words, "To Protect and Serve."

In a storybook South,
the plantation house has four tall columns,
Confederate battle flags fly from two rooftops
while men and women, dressed in white,
leisurely play croquet on the lawn.
In the distance,
the brown field is filled with dots of cotton,
a man walks beside a horse and bale-filled wagon,
not a slave in sight.

White faces fill every scene —

paintings and puzzles of privilege.

Native

Dakota, Choctaw, Wampanoag, Comanche —
names that echo off canyon walls,
blow in the wind over prairies,
rise fiercely from flames of burned villages
in smoke as ephemeral as government promises.

Warriors, weavers, hunters, herders,
once their drums were the heartbeat of a country
they called home
before they lost the land,
sacrificed it in trade for horses, guns,
measles, smallpox,
boundless land exchanged
for desolate reservations,
countless lives lost in vain,
even as the names live on
in places like
Ma-sa-chu-sett, Minnesota, Monongahela,
Tehachapi, Narragansett, Rappahannock.

As we breathe life into the names
every day
the land remembers.

Metaphor

Two young black men, barefooted,
joke and laugh
in the park near the condos.
From a distance,
they appear to be trying
to walk across something
like a tightrope,
strung between two trees.
One of them jumps up,
gets a foothold,
holds his arms out,
begins to carefully
walk toward his friend;
he teeters, catches himself,
places one foot in front of the other,
sways in the wind.

As I get closer,
I see that,
instead of rope,
they are walking on wide yellow
police caution tape,
stepping carefully,

trying to keep their balance.

Fault Lines

Sometimes
there is no doubt,
like when the tennis ball
lands clearly outside
the white boundary
or the car in back of you
smashes your bumper
at a stop sign.

Other times
it's muddled,
like when the deadly fire
consumes the warehouse
that wasn't properly inspected,
a shelter for homeless, drug users
and faulty appliances.

Or like the couple who sit across
from each other
in the attorney's office,
sign divorce papers,
each one blaming the other,

or the chasm
between political parties,
when all the What-Ifs
go round and round from talking heads,
as we keep looking for answers,
for someone to take responsibility
for anyone to explain
clearly, once and for all,
how we allowed this
to happen.

Confession to Anne Frank

I am your Judas,
your traitor,
the betrayer of your secrets,
but I am not an anti-Semite.
What I did has nothing to do
with your yellow star, Torah,
or denial of The Divine;
what I did came from selfish fear
of the same Gestapo
that terrorized your dreams,
the ones who would accuse me
of complicity,
arrest me with the other employees,
send us all with you to Westerbork
if I didn't write that anonymous note
to expose your location.
Now, you haunt my dreams,
starved, skeletal, bald,
weak and broken,
a tattooed number on your arm
as you haul rocks, dig rolls of sod.
The world will remember your strength
and courage,
while my identity remains forever hidden,
but I want you to know this:
I speak your name on the third day
of every September,
the day you boarded the final transport
headed to Auschwitz.
I speak your name, and for you,
I say Kaddish.

Upward Climb

I.
There is comfort
in a familiar stairway.
Our feet naturally fit
the smooth, worn indentations;
we read the history
of this place
through our soles,
grab the hand rail for support,
know where to avoid
squeaks or splinters,
climb with assurance of
what lies ahead.

II.
At Ellis Island,
an examiner tested immigrants
with a question of logic,
required them to explain
the best way to clean a stairway —
start at the bottom
or start at the top?
And the young girl answered
that she didn't come
to America to wash stairs,
which was a sensible response
back then,
when newcomers felt more
of a welcoming promise,
when an upward climb
still seemed possible.

War Is Not Healthy for Children

From the nearby recruiting office
they run through our neighborhood,
these boys who want to be men,
shirts off, baggy gym shorts,
feet hitting pavement in rhythmic strides,
cadence regulated by chanting
one two left right
horns honk, people wave.

I want to stop them

ask them to think about this,
remind them that there's more to being
a sailor, soldier or marine
than simply boot camp,
being physically fit,
that running from insurgents in Kunar province
always mindful of IEDs
is different than a run down a quiet street
on this spring afternoon
dodging nothing
but
bicyclists.

Terezin

From Prague, it's a one-hour journey, heading northwest,
past corn, hops, blankets of neon yellow rapeseed,
blue Sudeten mountains in the distance;
from city traffic into farmland so idyllic
it's easy to understand how Czech Jews might accept
The Lie,
told they were going to a place that would protect them,
specially designated for musicians, writers and artists.

Not a death camp,
Terezin has its own evil legacy,
a sham showcase, a fabricated town,
a "model ghetto" for Red Cross visitors
who were shown a propaganda film of prisoners
in gardens, soccer arenas, orchestras, schools,
smiles on their faces.

Had these visitors looked more closely,
they would have seen that the room full of sinks
had no plumbing,
the walls at the firing range were stained with blood,
plaster baked goods and candies filled window displays
behind locked doors of make-believe shops.

The truth is visible in the crematorium and cemetery,
in prison cells that still smell of dampness and deceit,
in unheated sleeping barracks with three tiers
of wooden plank beds,
in a tiny, one-room synagogue, hidden upstairs,
inside a fortress of streets, buildings, and chestnut trees,
surrounded by brick walls and a moat.

The perpetrators of hate tried to convince the world
that Terezin was typical,
but it was a twisted truth.
Underneath the cosmetics, the artificial façade,
despite the large black-and-white letters
which proclaim *ARBEIT MACH FREI*,
hard work never brought freedom here;
this place was, truly, like all the others —
just one more death trap camp
in the midst of peaceful green fields,

just one more station
on the journey to death.

Laminectomy

Waiting in pre-op area,
multi-pastel colored curtain
pulled for minimal privacy,
wet, cold antibacterial cloths
rubbed carefully over skin.

Waiting for the physician's assistant,
clothing and shoes removed,
green cotton hospital gown tied in back,
warm blankets on legs,
blood pressure cuff on right arm.

Waiting for the anesthesiologist,
IV started on left arm,
patient data entered into nurse's computer,
permission papers signed,
neon yellow booties on both feet.

Waiting for transport to the OR,
small TV airs Capitol Hill testimony,
the chief executive portrayed
as racist, con man, cheat, liar, bully.

We hold hands,
he in the bed, me in the chair,
waiting for all this to be over,
waiting for Congress to show more backbone,
waiting for the sharp blade of justice
like the surgeon's scalpel,
to remove this obstruction.

NPR Reports

Russian tanks
roll across deserted roads,
grandmothers make Molotov cocktails
as I drive to Target.

A journalist in Kyiv
interviews a lawyer
who has never shot a gun
or thought he could
until now
as I drive to the postal center.

In Kherson,
families hide in parking garages,
a mother cries,
a dog barks,
as I head to the grocery store

while Ukraine bleeds out.

Hurricane Dogs

Stranded in trees and on rooftops,
some, tethered still, to second-story balconies,
they silently observe the rescue boats go by,
listening to shouts,
looking for familiar faces,
their houses, now islands
surrounded by fetid floodwater

and I wonder why it is
that we grow numb
viewing the human tragedy
yet are moved to tears
at the sight of these pets,
abandoned
helpless,
while we sit in dry comfort
thousands of miles distant,
watching.

Their silence speaks to us
about making sacrifices
in a time of hard choices,
about waiting patiently,

about staying ever hopeful.

Internment

Manzanar sleeps
in the arid man-made desert
of Owens Valley.
Once home to thousands of displaced Japanese,
there is little left but cement foundations,
permanent scars that reveal a desolate story —
one square mile of wooden barracks,
walls of black tarpaper,
communal latrines and bedrooms with no partitions,
a camp that divided *them*
from us.

Today,
wind blows over loose sand and sage brush,
gardens and ponds are dry,
schools, cherry trees, rose bushes
have disappeared,
guard towers with machine gun mounts
and searchlights
the indelible proof that any idea of freedom here
was simply
a mirage.

Looking for America

> *I'm empty and aching, and I don't know why,*
> *Counting the cars on the New Jersey Turnpike,*
> *They've all come to look for America.*
> — PAUL SIMON

America,
how did you get lost?
We were all together,
walking toward
the same destination,
holding hands,
marching, singing,
until you let go,
turned the wrong way,
and we were pulled apart,
separated.

It happened so fast,
we must not have been
paying attention,
weren't watching you carefully
in the crowd
among all the yelling and distractions;
one minute you were there,
and then we lost sight of you.

Our biggest fear
is that you've been kidnapped
by domestic terrorists
armed with guns and disinformation,
false patriots
who refuse to hear the truth,
who will stop at nothing to thwart justice,
hold you hostage.

But perhaps
you have simply lost your way,
turned right when you should have gone left.
Maybe you can retrace your steps,
find your way back
to where you started.

And if that doesn't work,
don't worry;
lots of people are looking,
searching through empty promises,
abandoned ideals,
wasted opportunities, lost causes,
unfulfilled dreams,

and we will find you again

somewhere.

Baltimore: April 29, 2015

Inside Camden Yards
when the Orioles played the White Sox
on this idyllic spring afternoon,
the wail of sirens accompanied pre-game music
echoing across 46,000 empty seats,
while a few loyal followers hung banners,
looked on from nearby balconies,
gathered outside locked gates,
stood to watch through a wrought iron fence,
even as residents just blocks away swept up streets and stores
after days of riots, protest marches, curfew,
despair and frustration.
No vendors sold beer, hot dogs or peanuts,
no lines snaked toward restrooms,
no hawkers roamed the aisles with cotton candy,
lemonade or ice cream;
on the field, the players seemed smaller,
like Little League kids without parents in the bleachers,
surprised to hear their own voices
carry across the outfield to call for a catch
or encourage each other,
one player tossing a ball into the stands
to invisible spectators
where it rattled around like a huge pinball machine.
Through all nine innings,
the one constant sound was the sharp *slap*
of the ball into the catcher's mitt,
a loud *whack* we hear only rarely during a regular game,
a sound like a club hitting flesh,
yet rhythmic and strong
like the heartbeat of a city
as it slowly catches its breath.

31

Just Desserts

It took hours to make that pie,
to peel, pare, slice the apples,
mix flour, shortening, salt,
roll out the dough,
bake in the oven —
a crisp homemade crust,
gooey cinnamon fruit inside
a pyrex pie plate
placed on the roof of our car
temporarily,
then forgotten once we
slammed car doors,
rounded each curve all the way down
that windy Oakland hill
aptly named Snake Drive,
the plate hanging on somehow
until the very last turn,
when it flew off,
shattered on the asphalt,
glass and pie in pieces

and me not sure if I should
laugh or cry.

Crime Scene

Early this morning
there was a murder in our house
downstairs

witnessed by no one

but the evidence was scattered
throughout several rooms
filled, now, with feathers
like tiny gray petals
strewn across tile and carpet,
so soft and weightless
that my slippered footsteps
or small gasps of horror
sent them airborne
once more,
floating for a few seconds
across the silent kitchen

no sound but the refrigerator,
humming and purring
contentedly,

like

the

cat.

The Rat in the Bird Feeder

For at least a year
you remained a clever phantom,
although our next-door neighbor
swears he saw you, once,
run along the top of the fence,
and I have heard suspicious rustlings
near the composter
but preferred to think it was a young mourning dove,
like the one who hid in the ivy for days
until it could fly.

Sometimes, our cat would sit on the grass,
stare at the fence as if in a trance,
perhaps hearing your tiny movements,
but still, you were unconfirmed until this week
when (not once but twice) you brazenly appeared
right out in the open, gorging yourself on birdseed
from the feeder that hangs in the birch tree.
From our kitchen window, your soft, suede-like brown
resembled a bird's feathers, and we had to look twice
to make sure we were seeing
what we thought we were seeing.
And, when we approached quietly,
your flying leap back into the ivy was impressive
and very bird-like

but you aren't fooling anybody.

II.
Clever, aren't you,
to chew a hole through hard plastic,
burrow into the composter,
feast on apple parings, orange rinds,
curled leaves of Brussels sprouts,
remnants of red leaf lettuce.
These cold winter days keep you hidden,
but composted morsels continue to disappear,
so I have begun to feed you tasty tidbits on purpose,
throwing in an occasional piece of cheese
with the radish tops, cucumber skin,
egg shells and coffee grounds,
and before we left on vacation
my husband asked, "Have you fed the rat?"

Pathetically, now that the cat has died,
you have become our only pet.

Please Don't Hold a Carwash for My Funeral

Whose idea was this anyway?
It's so blatantly suspect,
always young girls, standing on the corner near a gas station,
wearing halter tops and cut-offs, shouting at passing cars,
holding poster boards with photos of the alleged deceased.
They certainly don't look bereaved,
and do we know this family member is *really* dead,
not just sitting at home
waiting,
hoping the relatives will seduce the sympathies
of enough suckers
to afford a new HD-TV
or at least a buffet dinner at Golden Corral?
Shouldn't we demand some kind of proof,
other than a collage of photos showing someone
smiling and very much alive?

I'm sorry.
I just don't buy it.

So after I'm gone,
if you truly don't have enough money
to turn me into ashes,
please consider other alternatives
like selling my clothes on eBay,
or telling the story to a newspaper human interest columnist.
Don't don your bikini
with that push-up bra,
yell at motorists
please…

I would die Hof embarrassment.

The Remains

"The vandals then danced upon the stump!"
— JOHN MUIR, CIRCA 1853

Near the beginning of the North Grove Trail
in Calaveras Big Trees
stands the remnant of an Earth wonder
and monument to man's greed —
the remains of what was once
a giant among giant Sequoias,
a majestic tree that towered almost
three hundred feet into Sierra Nevada sky,
left alone for twelve hundred years
until it was stripped of bark,
felled with wedges, pump augers
and avarice,
exploited as a money-making exhibition,
the bark re-formed into its original shape for display,
the fallen trunk used for a two-lane bowling alley
and bar,
the lower part planed smooth
so former gold miners and tourists
could say that,
although they never saw this colossal tree
when it stood in the forest,
they have now danced on the surface of its stump,

and isn't that even better?

Dust

Along with almonds, peaches, walnuts and grapes,
this valley grows dust.
Not the sensible, obedient dust
I knew in Long Beach
when my mother was keeping house,
this dust is stubborn,
sneaky,
somehow managing to work its way back inside
even double-paned windows,
insidiously coating everything
with a thin layer of film
just hours after I have wiped clean each surface,
wishing for a fixative to spray on,
to keep it just like this
for one more day.

Come into my house anytime,
lean down,
turn your head sideways,
pull your finger across a wooden shelf,
look for the evidence
that proves
we have met an unbeatable
enemy.

At the Edge

The shrill cry
pierced the hot, afternoon air,
a sound unmistakable
yet unexpected and rarely heard
in this busy neighborhood not far from the mall.

The two of us ran to the nearest window,
looked to the top of our tall redwood tree
just in time to see the hawk
taking flight again,
a crow in its talons,
swooping low over our roof
then lower still over the street,
majestic wings pushing down, lifting up,
struggling, momentarily,
with the heavy weight it carried,
then soaring once again,
flying northward
leaving us
almost awestruck

all in a matter of seconds,
our comfortable complacency shattered,
reminding us that once
not so long ago,
this land was a vineyard
where predators thrived,
before we became the trespassers
who paved the roads and shut our doors,
forgetting that the wildness
still lurks, always,
right at the edge.

Dear NPR,

Although I am a monthly donor,
your fund drives still cause feelings of guilt,
make me feel I should give more
since the car radio is tuned to you
ninety-five percent of the time,
unless I'm listening to a Giants game
or switch to Oldies instead of Marketplace
when Kai Ryssdal talks about trade deficits
and the stock market.
But it's not just the fund drives
that cause emotional distress;
it's programs like Radiolab and This American Life
which often interfere with my daily errands,
times when I am so involved with the story
I sit and listen in the parking lot
before getting on with my grocery shopping,
like today, when some Australian guy told a story
about his friend who was bitten three times
by a deadly tiger snake
in the middle of a presentation for school kids,
and since I was almost home
but didn't want to sit in the garage for another five minutes
to find out what happened,
I decided to drive slowly around the block,
not once but twice,
as I waited to hear the end.

I wondered what my son might think
if, for some reason,
he opened the "Find Friends" app on his phone
to see my current location,
watched my progress as the little icon
went round and round,
making seemingly mindless circles
on his screen.

The Missing Piece

The wheel of the stroller hit a rock,
causing me to look down just for a moment,
and that's when I saw it:
a jigsaw puzzle part,
blue, clean and bright
like a tiny piece of the sky,
lying strangely in an untidy flowerbed
caught, camouflaged among weeds.
I wondered how it got there
and when its loss would first be noticed,
the family around a card table,
all the other pieces carefully laid out and arranged by color,
picked up and fit correctly, one by one,
each in its proper place
until none was left,
yet still this one empty space
would remain
forever incomplete.

And I was reminded, once again,
of how the smallest things
can cause our lives, sometimes,
to fall softly out of control
with solutions in places we'd never think to look,
leaving holes that can never be filled
and images that will never be
exactly
as we had imagined.

Crows

The crows are displaced.

I see them in the neighborhood
looking oddly out of place,
strutting on driveways,
drinking awkwardly from sprinkler heads,
foraging in the gutters,
swooping down on lawns in groups of twos and threes.

At dawn's break they awaken us
with raucous cawing,
as though they are angry at all of us,
as if we had anything to do with ripping out the trees,
plowing under the corn,

building all the houses.

The Truth about Santa

I named her Carol,
since she was given to me on Christmas,
lashed eyes that opened and closed,
molded vinyl hair, pink bonnet covered,
the size of an actual three-month old,
substitute sister for an only child,
an eight-year-old's dream come true.

I wrapped her in a blanket,
carried and cradled her for hours,
no one suspecting the truth:
I had found her three weeks before,
the distinctive "Madame Alexander" blue box
hidden in the back of a closet
where I carefully lifted the lid,
parted pink tissue paper,
gently touched her face and legs,
secretly smelled her newness —
waited with holiday anticipation
for her to be wrapped as a gift
from my parents.

Instead
she appeared under the tree
with blue eyes open wide,
a small baby rattle placed in her dimpled fingers,
and even as I picked her up for the first time,
there was something bittersweet
in knowing the tag,
"From Santa,"
was a lie.

Orphans

Nestled in my jewelry box
one atop the other
are the earring orphans,
widows without mates,
survivors who somehow hung on
when their matching twin was
dropped carelessly to the ground
in a restaurant, theater, grocery store
as a scarf or sweater was removed;
abandoned,
they await the time when I am
eccentric, elderly, or both,
when I will wear the purple
dangle in my right ear,
the enamel red hoop in my left,
and no one will know for sure
if I have lost my senses
or simply decided to
flaunt convention,
or celebrate diversity.

To the Young Man Whose Invitation I Declined

Surely,
this must have been a joke
or maybe a dare;
if I had looked around
more carefully
maybe I would have seen
a friend of yours,
doubled over with laughter
somewhere near the entrance
to the gym,
because you couldn't have been serious
when you ran after me
as I hurried to my car,
perspiration on the back of my shirt,
saggy skin below black acrylic work-out shorts
that do not reveal a small, tight, youthful ass.
"Could I take you to lunch sometime?"
you asked,
as if this were something I hear every day,
as if you honestly expected I would say yes,
and I was so astonished, I blurted out
the first thing that came to mind,
something about being married,
nothing about all the questions I thought of later,
the most obvious
simply being
WHY?

Reprimand*

You know, Moon,
I've gotta draw the line this time.
There really is such a thing as
being too ostentatious,
too full of yourself,
and I'm sure you were hoping
that all of us writers
would look at this painting,
find words to praise you,
pen rhymed words about how you inspire
lovers, werewolves and lunatics,
how you pull the tides,
always hide your Dark Side,
but I'm not going to do it this time
because this is simply too much,
too hard to believe,
and while we're on the subject,
I'd like to remind you that your
fine, flour-like dust is lethal,
your true colors are dull grays,
you would never look luminescent
if it weren't for the sun,
and as far as I know,
only twelve people have ever visited you
in person.

*In response to the oil
painting "Moon Madness"
by Andrew Wyeth.*

What has happened

to the yardstick
that always hangs in the closet
under the stairs,
the small, heavy bolt
that was left right there
on the Delft blue bedroom carpet
under the unfinished inversion table,
the narrow hand shovel
that's always on the potting bench
or in a flowerbed,
and the hammer
which has its own designated spot
above the garage workbench —
all mysteriously disappeared
within the past week,
no signs, no clues,
and no sightings of the miniature
household gnomes
who no doubt need all these items
for a major project —
a much more pleasant notion
than that of a burglar unlatching the back gate at night,
sneaking into our yard, garage, house,
or worse yet
that we have simply misplaced
or accidentally thrown away
all these items
ourselves
and have no recollection
whatsoever.

Science Lesson

"They only live two weeks, anyway,"
the teacher explained,
as though to ease my daughter's mind
and lessen our guilt as we served as accomplices
in this crime,
searching for insects all afternoon,
overturning rocks and logs,
trapping with a net,
each specimen carefully placed in a zip-lock bag,
sentenced to live out final hours breathing fumes
from acetone-soaked cotton balls.

"Find samples from seven different classifications,"
the teacher directed,
and so we categorized,
the sandwich bags grouped in neat piles on our counter,
protestations buzzing from fly, bee, and wasp,
moths and butterflies fluttering delicate wings
in dignified desperation,
while the potato bug (Jerusalem cricket / *Stenopelmatus fuscus*),
nudged and pushed unceasingly against his plastic prison seal,
gnawing an escape route,
chewing for three days without food,
taking tiny insect bites of clear polyethylene
until at last he was free…
only to struggle up the slippery sides of a stainless steel bowl.
Such determination.
But then again, not surprising for a creature
with so short a life.
If you had only two weeks to live,
wouldn't you want to
take some risks?

Notre Dame

I.
Our Dear Lady,
it seems that all of France
and much of the world
has wept over your latest tragedy.
At the risk of stating the obvious,
I would like to remind you
that an existence of 850-plus years
is likely to be filled with its share of ups and downs.
The temptation, of course, is to always
focus on the positive memories...
the coronations, Requiem Masses,
the delightful tight rope walk between the bell towers,
not to mention the alleged relics from the crucifixion...
so let's not pretend this fire
is the worst thing that has happened.
Let's also remember the funerals,
the suicides at the altar,
the revolution when your statues were beheaded
and you were converted to a mundane warehouse
for the storage of food.
Don't forget that it was the fictitious story
of a lonely hunchback
that brought attention to your woeful plight,
saved you from destruction,
supported you in a time of great need
(even more than your flying buttresses),
and even in the midst of liberation
from your German foes,
stray bullets shattered stained glass from the Middle Ages.

So, it's difficult
to summon much sympathy.
After all, at significant expense,
you have had an ongoing makeover,
centuries of facelifts and joint replacements;
you have been cleaned, refreshed, updated,
pampered and revered,
and no doubt you will once again
rise above us all.

II.
After some consideration,
I fear I may have maligned you unfairly.
Compared to the multiple misfortunes and afflictions
you have experienced over the centuries,
this devastating fire seemed, at first,
to be simply one more challenge
you would undoubtedly overcome —
that you would recover completely
and be back to your old self in no time.
The latest prognosis, I'm forced to admit,
looks far less hopeful,
and I can only imagine your distress
at being told there is a mere fifty-fifty
chance of your survival.

Since, after all, you are a cathedral,
I would urge you to look toward the Heavens
for some kind of divine intervention,
and please take some comfort,
as we Americans so often do,
in our sincere thoughts and prayers.

Eulogy

Within one year
she lost her mother
her husband
and her Siamese cat.

Sadly
it was the cat
she missed the most.

Of the three,
he was the only one
who really ever
listened.

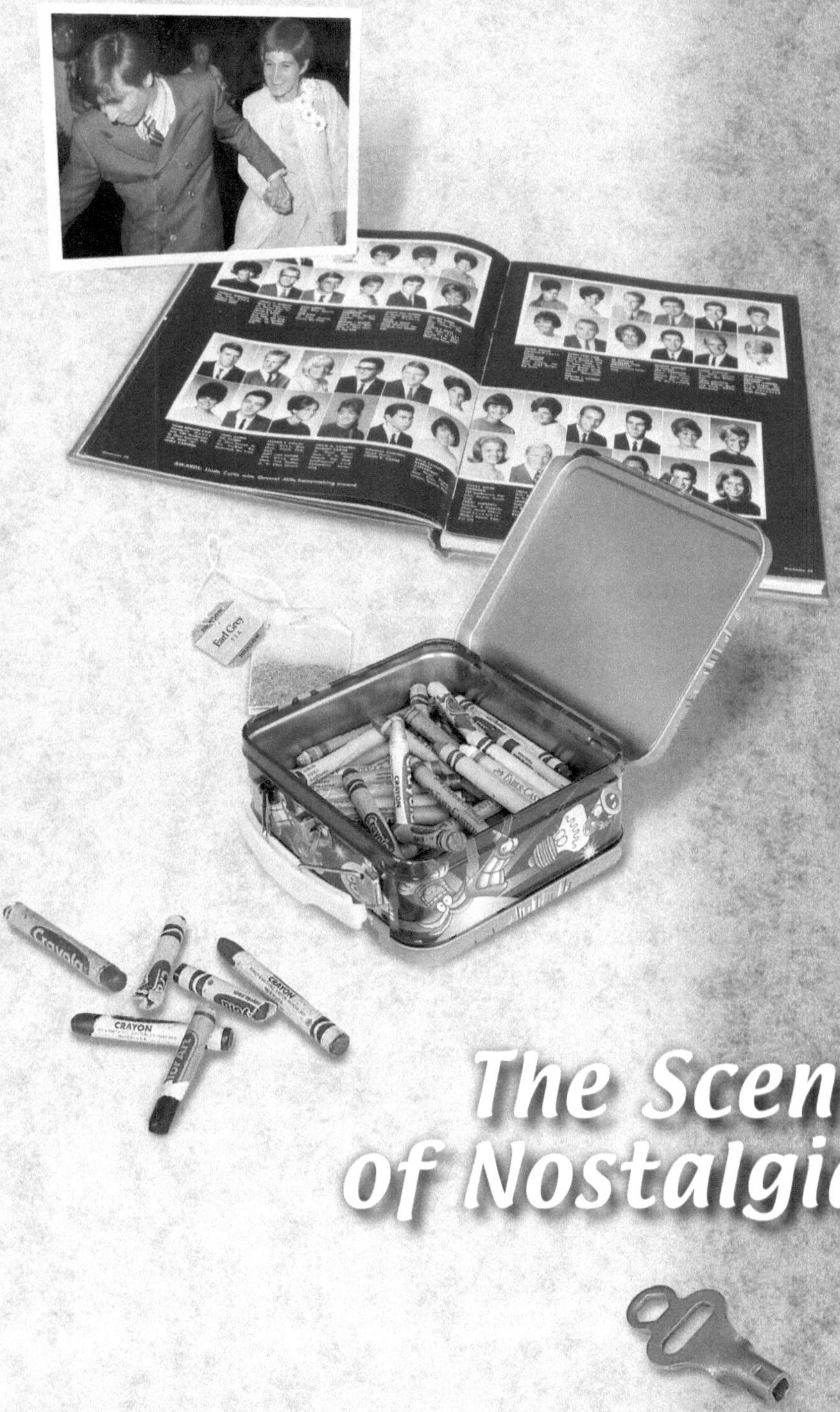

The Scent of Nostalgia

Sunriver

We rode our bikes past the house where my father died,
our bodies unconsciously leaning to the right slightly,
just for a second,
as if to turn up the familiar lava rock driveway,
drop the kickstands and walk to the front door
where heavy leaded glass creates wavy images
into rooms we know so well —
the feel of tightly-woven Berber carpet
on summer's bare feet,
the smoothness of the wooden banister and windowsills,
how the hummingbirds hover at the feeder's sultry sweetness
above the patio bench,
and the way snow blankets the redwood deck,
weighing down nearby pines and junipers heavy white.

By now, the new owners undoubtedly know
how the water comes from the tap ice cold and pure
even on the hottest August day,
how an evening wind carries the sounds of train whistles
and yelping coyotes,
and the way it feels to stand outside in winter stillness
under the silence of a million stars.

What they will never know
is the sound of our laughter,
the footsteps of our children running up and down the stairs,
the clock that chimed every half hour,
marking the time we spent together,
twice each year,
when this house was our home.

Fifty years later

he remembers the jacket, smell of the leather,
the way the fringe hung off the sleeves,
remembers the apartment in the Haight district,
Jefferson Airplane posters on the walls,
oversized pillows on the floor,
thrift shop sofa singed with cigarette burns,
how they cringed at middle class values,
unhinged the bedroom door,
hung long strings of beads that clicked together,
caught morning light,
how they binged on soda crackers, peanut butter,
cheap wine.
On quiet evenings
the girl sang as she played her mandolin.

Doppelganger

The cramped boutique
sells items from another era:
fragrant soaps, hats, gloves, pins,
an assortment of small filigree frames
displayed on a table,
each filled with a sepia photo, circa 1900.
In one, a young girl holds a small flag in her left hand,
a lacy parasol in the other,
a kind of sailor hat askew on her head,
white blouse with high Victorian collar,
her neck completely covered.
She faces the camera not quite smiling,
just an ordinary girl,
except that she looks so much like my daughter
they could be twins,
one born a hundred years earlier
who knew button shoes, long skirts,
gas lights, Tiffany glass —
an exact replica of my twentieth century child.

I can't stop staring.
I must buy the photograph,
place it in my own wooden frame,
hang it on the wall near her bedroom door —
a ghost daughter
with arched eyebrows, shadowed eyes
who looks sideways at us
day after day at the top of the stairs,
a knowing expression on her face

like she has a secret.

Scented Nostalgia

A woman behind me, in line at the grocery store —
I smell her cologne.
For a moment it eludes me,
then evokes a memory
of pastel packaged bubble bath,
small paper envelopes,
in a bathroom with a heater on the wall.
Sometimes I would turn out all the lights,
sit on the terry cloth rug,
watch the coils glow in the warmth of childhood.

Bookstore browsing,
turning glossy pages,
an unfamiliar book — yet somehow familiar —
I knew this same smell years ago:
high school yearbook,
pages reserved, messages written,
promises to stay in touch with friends
whose names now appear unfamiliar
on reunion rosters.

My daughter's seventh birthday —
a newly-opened box of crayons,
a smell unchanged for years
brings no distinct recollection,
just the essence of innocence
for a moment,
recaptured.

Classic Blue*

It's one of the last photos
in our white Hallmark album,
both of us running away from the church,
heads down, smiling,
hands clasped together,
toward our car and honeymoon.

In the fifty years
since that night in September,
the Kodachrome colors have faded,
dimmed the dress I wear in the picture,
but I'm sure it was classic blue,
sleeveless, with white daisies appliquéd around the hem
like the daisies that decorated my wedding dress,
and the real ones in the corsage pinned to my sheer coat,
lightweight and lacy
to show off the vibrant blue underneath.

We hadn't gone far from the church
when we pulled into the parking lot
of an IHOP or Denny's;
too nervous to eat much before the ceremony,
we realized we were hungry,
took a seat in the padded booth,
laughed as we shook rice from our hair and clothes,
twisted the new rings on our fingers.

Pantone's Color of the Year

William

At eighteen months
my grandson has already learned
to be brave.
Grandpa says wait here
I'll be right back
and disappears into the garage —

alone
momentarily abandoned,
taking big gulps,
lower lip quivering,
but no tears,
he stands in the backyard
holding only a shovelful
of trust.

Shadows and Reflections

My mother's face and voice,
once as familiar
as my own signature
or the soothing sound of rain,
have become memories yellowed with age,
like the lace on the gown
she sewed for my wedding;
dimmed like old photographs
no longer vibrant with color,
her aspects elude me even as
I run my fingers down the surface
of an oil painting,
searching for the softness of the hand
that created it.

Today, in this year that divides
our thirty-two years together
from thirty-two years apart,
I look for traces of her in my own reflection,
catching a glimpse, sometimes,
in the gray of my hair,
the slight swell of my belly,
more often seeing shadows of my father
in the set of my jaw
the turn of my mouth,
and I worry she is lost to me
until I find her again,
just for a moment
in my daughter's smile.

1967

We were seniors in high school,
a weekend retreat for honor students,
a camp in Angeles National Forest.
Instead of our studies,
what I remember best
is sitting together in front of a stone fireplace
late at night,
just our teacher and the two of us
warmed by the flames;
the next morning
we ran through deep snow together —
the first time you held my hand.

That night,
I was in a top bunkbed,
small window perfectly placed
to stare outside
at the magic of my first snowfall,
too excited to sleep,

enchanted.

My son knows death

knows its power,
its duplicity,
how it can be both desired
and feared,
both merciful and cruel,
how it can move slowly
or strike without warning.

During this time of plague,
his office sits directly across
a corridor of closed doors,
each room an isolated cell
for a victim of the virus;
IV pumps and monitors
outside each door,
extra long tubing snaking inside,
keeping contact to a minimum.
No touching.
No family.
No visitors
except Death
who is always there,
silent, unseen,
the most powerful presence
in that hallway.

Liquid Alchemy

Standing at the kitchen counter,
I tear open the small packet of Earl Grey
inhaling deeply,
breathing in the essence of Britain
before dunking the bag up and down
into steaming water,
creating no ordinary cup of tea
but a magic concoction
which transports me back to The Orangery,
Kensington Gardens,
my first afternoon in London,
clichéd and complete with scones
and a light rain.

The details of that day
are preserved and returned to me
as I close my eyes and sip
this soothing liquid,
this powerful potion.

Requiem for Scott

His parents drove in silence,
parked their car
near the spot where his abandoned truck
had been found.
Once they carried hope,
fragile and soft,
as weeks became months;
it whispered not to give up
until now

now that hikers had discovered his remains,
now that fragments had been unearthed
now that the truth had been found
in pieces under their feet.

They walked through the forest
over a pine needle carpet
thick enough to keep a secret
buried for seven months,
offering no answers,
nothing that would explain
how their son, also a father,
could leave to meet someone on a hot July afternoon
and never return.

Perhaps it is a bond that is never broken,
a connection between mother
and first-born;
perhaps that would explain why,
as she walked in ever widening circles,
eyes looking always down,
she found another bone,
overlooked by all the investigators,
a rib bone,
a bone she once nourished with her body
as he grew under her own rib
so close to her heart,
so many years ago
when the future held such promise.

Handed Down

Drab olive-green cotton,
the heavy field jacket
hung in a closet for years.
My grandson wears it now;
a lover of history,
excited to find an old candy wrapper
in one of the pockets,
he explains that it came from an Israeli company
which sent chocolates to soldiers,
tells me this is an M1943 jacket,
my dad's paratrooper wings
pinned on the front lapel.

My dad told stories of the war,
most of them humorous,
filled with a love of places
he always wanted to visit again
but never did.
I wish I had recorded his stories
before the Alzheimer's cobwebbed them,
so my grandson could hear them now,
feel like he was there in the same room
with his great-grandfather,
the two of them sitting near the wood-burning stove
the jacket linking them together.

Watching A Hard Day's Night Fifty Years Later

It's the film I would sneak in to see
over and over on Saturday afternoons in 1964,
sitting with friends in plush theater seats for eighty-eight
tantalizing minutes before fidgeting
through the second feature
(almost always "Ferry 'Cross the Mersey"),
walking back to the lobby when it ended,
mingling cleverly with the incoming horde of teenage girls,
turning back around to find a new seat
where we could watch again
until we knew the lines by heart,
whispered them to ourselves as the scenes played,
dreamed of meeting each Beatle in person,
practiced a British accent,
tried to dress like the girls on the screen,
wrote stories filled with kisses and naive romantic references
in our beginning time.

Seeing them now,
I am astonished at their youth,
their optimism and joy of performing
simple harmonies and straightforward lyrics,
before the world recognized their genius,
before *Sgt. Pepper* and *Let It Be*,
before the weariness of travel, drugs, fights over money,
before Yoko, cancer, and Mark David Chapman —
they are that new 45 record we couldn't stop playing,
the new piece of sheet music carried home
in the vellum envelope;
they are fresh, genuine,
captured forever in black and white,
in their beginning time.

Obituary

It was her name that first caught my eye
in the daily obituaries:
Dianna Spencer,
like the princess of Wales,
a native of Sacramento, age fifty-two,
survived by her mother.
No husband.
No children.
The notice read
She was a carnival worker for twelve years.
She enjoyed collecting Elvis memorabilia,
as though this were the main focus of her life,
and maybe it was,
but really
is this how she would want to be remembered?
Is there nothing more that could have been written,
some mention of richness in her life,
not just allusions to tacky paintings on black velvet
or statuary knick-knacks?
Surely, she must have known love.
I'd like to think there was someone for her.
Maybe the man, Harley-tattooed,
who worked the balloon dart booth next to hers
and wanted to take her away from their small-town life,
perhaps someone like him saw the goodness in her heart,
thought of her as the one he wanted to come home to,
the one who could be
his Graceland.

The immigrant in 1900

knows steerage and squalor,
suspenders, shirts of heavy ticking,
labors in a Lower East Side sweatshop
filled with the droning of machines, smell of new leather.
He dines on potatoes, cabbage, bread,
an occasional apple or turnip,
strolls on Sunday past Delancey Street delicatessens
offering pastrami, knishes, borscht, bagels,
while pushcarts proffer pickles, baskets, door hinges and more.
He walks down Mulberry Street to Chinatown,
wanders among live goats, pig carcasses, perfume of incense.

He dreams the American Dream,
the dream of men who stay at the Fifth Avenue Hotel,
the ones who smoke cigars, use brass spittoons,
wear gold fobs draped across silken vests,
bowler hats and stiff white collars,
spat-style boots with buttons on the side,
shoes he cobbles but can't afford.

He dreams of the Adriatic Sea,
cerulean coastal waters below his home in Ancona
before the Passage, before Ellis Island;
in his sleep, he takes a spoonful of brodetto,
tastes the oil, garlic, saffron, the pecorino cheese,
walks along the Italian beach in bright sunlight,
then opens his eyes in a New York tenement
as winter snow falls.
He rolls over,
dreams again.

A New Beginning

On our way to shop at the sutlers' tents
we pass through the artillery camp,
horses in a line on our left,
each almost identical to the next,
dark brown glossy coats,
long black manes and tails.

Not so long ago,
these Standardbred horses
trotted and paced in harness races,
pulled carts in front of grandstands, noisy crowds,
until their stride and winnings diminished,
their futures expendable.

Today,
they pull limbers, caissons, cannons
in teams of four and six
at this reenactment of history;
like synchronized dancers
they move as one,
joined in harnesses that clink and rattle
as they respond to reins and commands,
rush supply wagons, Civil War ambulances,
then stand strangely calm when artillery concussions
shake the ground.

Some wait their turn
as we walk by,
watch with alert brown eyes
focused on the wagon and four-horse team
circling the field without them;
others stand with knees locked,
sleep in the sun.

And now they dream
of charges into battle's chaos,
of smoke that fills the field,
the shouts of men in blue
who have rescued them,
provided a second chance,
a new beginning
in this Union "Army."

Sometimes I mourn the loss of fog

which hung like a curtain
outside winter windows;
not transparent sheers,
but thick gray-white drapes
that obstructed views,
closed us in,
muffled sounds,
hid the nearby orchards and vineyards
transformed, now,
into neighborhoods
which cover the soil,
hold on to sunlight and heat,
suck up moisture,
repel vapor.

In its way,
that fog was reassuring,
whispering the message
that, although we lived
with the usual creature comforts,
we were still close to the earth
somehow,
not just one more subdivision
amid suburban sprawl.

November, 1963

What I remember most
is the drumbeat —
slow, steady, rhythmic,
like the heartbeat of a nation in mourning.
A cadence of grief
accompanied by caisson wheels turning,
jangling of stirrups on a riderless horse,

the profound silence of the crowd

as the funeral cortege made its way
toward Arlington,
past those who lined the streets,
the rest of us watching our televisions
in shock
and overwhelming sadness
for the children,
the veiled widow
walking with grace and dignity
between the two brothers.

There would be other processions like this
in later years,
but this was the first for me —
bringing with it great losses
of trust
of life
of innocence.

Final Evaluation

Throughout nearly four decades of teaching,
administrators have routinely observed,
judged,
required objectives,
looked for active participation,
standards and goals written on the board —
tangible, verifiable results
to prove I was doing my job.

Throughout those same
bell-regimented months and semesters
I have played that game,
thanked them for their accolades,
pretending it was all about
delivery of content,
test scores,
but knowing it was really about inspiring creativity,
boosting confidence
and teaching values that cannot be tested
with multiple choice questions.

And in the dozens of yearbooks
boxed and stored in the dormers of my house
are signatures and personal messages,
thank you letters from hundreds of students —
notes never shared with any principal,
yet I consider them
above all else,
to be my
genuine
final
evaluation.

Gardenias

During the summer of 1964
when I was fifteen,
I left the overcast beaches of southern California
for the welcome warmth of Yuba City,
to the ranch home of my aunt and uncle
where I lived like a princess
in a new addition to their house —
my own domain,
complete with private bath,
a round bed
and glass doors that opened to the backyard,
beckoning me to spend hours swimming in their pool,
listening to the radio,
sunning myself,
feeling, perhaps, for the first time
more like a teenager than a little girl.

Tonight, almost fifty years later,
I turn off the air conditioner,
open upstairs bedroom windows,
inhale the smell of blooming gardenias
and just for a moment
I am that young girl again
in that backyard
on the cusp of womanhood
breathing in fragrance and heat.

After the pandemic

we will remember
empty shelves of toilet paper,
hand sanitizer, paper towels,
antibacterial wipes,
juxtaposed with abundance of fear.

We will remember
empty parking lots,
months without baseball,
closed shopping malls, restaurants,
movie theaters, schools,
how we stood in long lines
to enter Trader Joes, Home Depot, Costco,
wore our masks everywhere.

I will remember
my daily walks,
and how everyone –
runners, dog walkers,
stroller pushers,
and other walkers like me –
crossed streets constantly
to avoid coming face-to-face
on the sidewalk,
sometimes waved,
often made no eye contact at all,

as though being invisible
could protect us.

An Only Child

Beach Memories

Warm summer sun,
Alamitos Bay calm waters,
Mama and I sat on an old cotton quilt,
ate tuna sandwiches wrapped in waxed paper,
drank lemonade from a plaid thermos,
sometimes a Fudgsicle or ice cream Drumstick
for dessert
from the Snack Shack
down the beach.

In the afternoons,
we made drip castles —
dug a large hole,
filled it with water,
wet the sand,
funneled the dark gray mixture through our fingers
like an invisible frosting tube,
layered heavy drops to form fragile walls and towers,
vulnerable and short-lived
like my childhood

at the edge of the sea.

Awaiting the Tooth Fairy

When I started to lose
my baby teeth,
Daddy tried,
time after time,
to tie a dental floss knot
around the wiggly tooth
or hold two fingers
inside one of his handkerchiefs
to get a better grip
but
I think because he was afraid of hurting me,
the tooth often ended up dangling,
bleeding
the roots unwilling to yield —
so I would go next door to visit Charlie,
a father of seven,
relying on his years of experience.

I can't recall his face,
yet I trusted this man,
his thumb and index finger in my mouth,
smelling and tasting of cigarettes,
so rough and different from my father's
as he bent down on one knee,
confidently grasped and pulled,
then wrapped each small tooth
in a paper towel or Kleenex,
my tongue filling the empty space as I walked home,

a prize to show my dad.

Ride 'Em Cowgirl

Ever mindful of children's growing feet,
my parents denied my desire for cowboy boots,
just as they also refused my request for a horse
to stable in our suburban Long Beach backyard,
so I straddled the wooden swing
next to the two-seat glider,
floppy red rubber rain boots pulled over my shoes,
a fringed vest and skirt over T-shirt and shorts,
fingers gripping the large chain links
instead of the pommel of a saddle
as I rocked back and forth
riding for miles.

Make Believe

An only child,
I created other worlds in my house:
closed all doors into the hallway,
made a long, quiet room
where I spread my mother's soft,
sour-smelling bamboo beach mat,
drank pretend tea from Japanese lacquerware cups,
clicked ivory chopsticks
to eat phantom meals;
or, on rainy nights,
I formed a make-believe camp
inside a covered wagon,
my top sheet and blanket
propped up with a majorette baton,
a flashlight reflecting off the dimples of cold steel
like sparks
of my imagination.

Crayola Memories

I.
My mother,
who delighted in using watercolors, oils, acrylics,
soon learned that a page from her sketchbook —
heavy, textured, and blank —
brought only frustration to me;
so we took old crayons,
small leftovers of brick red, burnt sienna,
midnight blue, sea green,
peeled off paper,
twisted the smooth nubbins
in a tiny pencil sharpener,
watched as colorful curls mounded on waxed paper
that we folded, pressed with a hot iron,
the hues melting and blending together,
to form an abstract painting
taped in a window
glowing like stained glass.

II.
My father,
who had a place for everything —
tools traced and hung in matched shapes
on the workbench wall,
paper clips, pencils, photos
neatly divided in tins and cigar boxes in his desk drawers —
gave me coloring books,
the images already drawn,
and he taught me how to outline,
to follow the pattern,
press the crayon around the edge
slightly darker,
then fill in the empty spaces
carefully, methodically,
the same way I learned to be a perfectionist,
to crave neatness, order,
to follow the rules,
to live my life
staying within the lines.

At Grandma Becky's

There were no doves in my suburban neighborhood,
but at my grandma's house on inner-city Gaviota Avenue,
their soft, repetitive cooing
would awaken me on weekend visits
into her back bedroom of flowered wallpaper —
the soft scent of lavender,
small, satin sachets
mingling with wild roses and berries
tangled in the backyard,
along with an undefinable odor
of oldness.

Lying in her double bed,
I would think about the hard molasses cookies
in large Mason jars,
old issues of *McCall's* magazines
behind glassed-in bookshelves,
an unfinished jigsaw puzzle on the dining table,
and the rhythmic creaking of her recliner,
reassuring me
always
of her presence.

3602 Petaluma Avenue

I.
In 1954,
all the houses were new,
a post-war neighborhood,
streets named alphabetically —
Knoxville, Ladoga, Monogram,
Nipomo, Ostrom, Petaluma —
front lawns seeded,
protected with stakes and string,
the smell of fertilizer strong in the air,
young trees in the parkways,
wide sidewalks smooth,
uncracked

invitation for roller skates.

II.
On chilly mornings,
I would stand over the grating
of our floor furnace in the hallway,
warm air ballooning my nightgown.

When it rained,
Mama set up a rack to dry clothes
near the same furnace
on the living room side,
sheets, towels, shirts, underwear,
draping over thin wooden rods,
decorating a colorful
accordion of laundry.

What Was I Thinking?

I'm pretty sure it happened during first grade
as we sat on the carpet,
listened to the teacher read a book.
I picked up a stray button that fit perfectly
into my nostril,
which, at the time,
seemed like an interesting thing to do
until I inhaled deeply, sniffed the button
too far back to reach with my finger,
every attempt only pushing it back even more.
I raised my hand,
asked permission to go to the bathroom,
ran in and strained on the toilet,
remembering a story my mother had told me
about another kid who swallowed a safety pin
and eventually forced it out in this manner,
but this procedure failed to produce instant results.
So I left the bathroom, ran across the playground,
went out the gate in the chain link fence,
ran all the way home,
surprised my mother who immediately called the school,
no one but me knowing the truth of what I'd done,
which I refused to divulge for hours,
ignoring my mother's worried looks
until my breathing began to suffer
and I admitted the deed,
was taken hastily to the doctor
who extracted the button with a special instrument,
told my mother that if it had gone on much longer
I would have needed surgery.

I don't remember being disciplined in any way,
though I could never explain why I had done
such a stupid thing

except that the button fit perfectly.

A Childhood Memory

Series of strep infections,
inflamed tonsils,
missed school days,
doctor visits,
a surgery,
pediatric ward,
high-railed beds,
ether dreams,
orange Aspergum,

like swallowing fire.

Wagon Train Girlhood

When I was eleven
my friend Diane
would play Wagon Train with me,
the front porch
transformed, for us, into a conestoga,
as we lifted our imaginary skirts to walk down
cement steps,
gathering twigs for firewood,
picking small, red pyracantha berries
to serve in plastic toy dishes —
berry stew
berry pudding
a side dish of purple, jacaranda blossoms.

Sometimes we galloped to the corner
on unseen horses,
looping invisible reins over the mailbox,
walking off to meet
a pretend husband
or pioneer scout lover,
our arms encircling the street lamp post,
lips kissing stone,
teeth brushing lightly
against the hard reality
of rough granite.

Dentists

As she trims my hair,
my stylist confesses she is on edge,
nervous about her upcoming dental appointment
later that afternoon;
she talks about her childhood dentist,
calls him a quack,
a sadist,
tells how he connected all her fillings,
laid a silver street in her mouth impenetrable to floss.
Once, she says, a client argued with her
about whose dentist was the worst,
only to find out they had both gone to the same man!

I try to remember my first dentist,
but even his name is forgotten;
what comes to mind
are Archie, Betty, Jughead and Veronica,
characters from comic books
that occupied my time as I waited to be called,
breathed an unidentifiable medicinal smell
in the cramped waiting room.
No anesthesia, gas, or novocaine;
instead, he would offer a forefinger
as he filled the cavities,
telling me to squeeze
if he caused any pain.

Made By Hand

My grandmother's sounds
were the snap and chop of pinking shears,
the treadle of the sewing machine
and hiss of the steam iron.
She perused the pattern books,
Butterick, Simplicity, McCall's,
selecting designs for my fall school wardrobe
while I watched the store clerk
turning the heavy fabric bolts,
laying the cloth against the yardstick on the table,
measuring and cutting,
folding the material into small, neat squares
that would later become
jumpers, dresses, blouses, vests,
my grandma's mouth full of straight pins
as I stood on a chair where she fitted and basted,
aligning a hem or changing a dart,
all the while never knowing that what I really wanted
were the dresses in the stores,
the ones like all the other girls wore,

the ones, I realize now,
that weren't made especially for me
with her love.

When I was nine

my father taught me baseball.
Not how to take a stance
and grip the bat
or slide into second base,
but how to listen —
to close my eyes and visualize
the game.

And we would lie on the floor
near the hi-fi
in the fading afternoon light,
screen door open,
cushioned atop the tiny loops
of our new, nylon wall-to-wall carpeting,
imagining every fastball
from Sandy Koufax,
every base stolen
by Maury Wills,
almost tasting the peanuts
and feeling the metal seats,
listening to Vin Scully
making it seem real
play by play

side by side

just the two of us,

together.

Boots

Cordovan colored leather work boots
heavy, clumsy,
the kind that laced up past the ankles,
the last thing I wanted to wear to sixth grade camp in 1961,
but Daddy drove me downtown, anyway, to Sears,
carried home the large, square shoe box tied with string.

I think my mother understood,
knowing, as we packed my suitcase,
that I would never put them on,
yet insisting I take the boots to make my father happy.

It was often like that between us —
awkward, slightly strained, somehow out of sync —
my dad always hoping he got it right
and I, unable to tell him otherwise,
his best intentions all too often ignored
like the boots
that stayed in the box
rarely ever worn
and now discarded.

Too late,
I realize these boots were a lot like my dad:
strong, sensible,
exactly what I needed,
meant to keep me upright

not slipping and falling.

Impatient

For the holiday that year,
Mama had used solid-color
wrapping paper in shades of red, green and white;
then, with a bottle of white paste,
she drew decorations on the top:
a tree, a candle, our names.
When the drawing was complete,
she held the package over newspaper,
sprinkled glitter that stuck to the paste,
to make a sparkling design.

For a reason I've long forgotten,
a particular present
was of great interest to me;
wrapped in red, with my name glittery on top,
it was stacked behind others under the tree.
When nobody was around,
I picked it up, took it into our small TV room,
carefully peeled off scotch tape,
somehow managed to unwrap enough
to look inside the shoebox
where my grandmother had carefully placed
handmade clothes for one of my dolls:
a blue flannel coat, lacy pinafore with matching blouse,
a small skirt with fabric that matched one of my own.

I'm sure I didn't rewrap the package carefully;
I'm sure my mother and grandmother
exchanged knowing looks but said nothing.
I still remember feeling guilty for snooping,

but I simply couldn't wait.

Roller Skates

You could say I literally skated through the 1950s,
schoolday afternoons and weekends
spent circling the block,
no helmet, kneepads
or iPhone earbuds,
just the percussive sound of ballbearings
on cement sidewalk,
the hard staccato rhythm as I pounded
over the cracks,
coveting my friends' smooth, white leather shoe skates,
riding instead on last year's black oxfords
clamped tightly to the expandable frame and wheels,
striding
pushing
gliding
jarring,
the skate key on a cord around my neck,
its shape just right to fit the curl of my tongue
as I flew along
experiencing the hard
metallic taste
of total freedom.

Carpool Karaoke

Memories from my Playlist

I.
Piano keys pound out first notes,
the Chiffons sing,
One fine day, you'll look at me,
and you will know our love was
meant to be…
and I am transported to 1963
in a diner with a tabletop juke box,
asking my dad for coins to play this song;
he winks at me,
wonders why I want to hear
an aria from Madame Butterfly,
knowing the titles are the same.

II.
Now it's Dan Fogelberg,
and when the chorus begins,
I am inside our van,
cross-country trip to Boston in 1994,
husband and daughter joining voices,
And the reach like a siren sings
as she beckons and calls…
played multiple times
through southwestern deserts,
on eastern turnpikes,
back again across the Rockies.

Same song,
twenty-four years later,
just two of us this time,
on a drive along the rocky coast
of Acadia National Park,
singing along with the timely lyrics:
It's Maine, and it's autumn,
The birches have just begun turning…

III.
The unmistakable voice of James Taylor
sings a cappella,
If I had stopped to listen once or twice,
if I had closed my mouth and opened my eyes…
a short song, one of my favorites,
but one I never expected to hear in person.
I can close my eyes,
remember our seats at Cal Expo,
picture him on the stage without his guitar,
a third or fourth encore,
as he takes a deep breath,
begins to sing,
while I stand and cry.

An Ode to Ice Cream

In a bowl, mug, cup,
atop a cone or piece of pie,
you are the universal panacea,
the Magic Bullet that soothes tears,
celebrates success,
improves the flavor of even the driest
cake, brownie or waffle;
you are a temptress in simple pink, white, or brown,
a seductive siren when accessorized with nuts, chips,
whipped cream, gooey hot fudge
slithering down your curves,
beneath a neon-red cherry.
We turn to you after our losses,
tonsillectomies, wisdom teeth removal,
the ninth inning walk-off wins by the opposing team;
in a universal language,
you never fail to bring comfort,
you own your richness,
stand strong against your competitors —
the ice milks, the yogurts —
for you are the original,
politically correct, diverse, multi-colored,
down home like butter pecan,
childish like chocolate chip cookie dough,
refreshing like green tea,
and always exactly right

like plain chocolate and vanilla.

Carpool Karaoke

Four of us in the car
heading south to Irvine
in typical L.A. congestion
which quickly evolves into
stop-and-go,
no end in sight.

To pass the time as we inch along,
one of us suggests we sing
songs from Broadway musicals,
so we start with *West Side Story*,
on to *My Fair Lady*,
Sound of Music,
Les Mis.

Windows rolled down,
we belt out tunes
like theater performers,
oblivious to the stares
from travelers around us,
amaze ourselves with the lyrics
we can remember,
forgetting our slow progress.

An hour later,
we arrive at our destination,
brother and sister-in-law
anxious to hear all the news,
but after our car concert,
our family quartet can hardly talk.

Abbey Road

I.
My granddaughters think it's some kind of magic,
how I know which song comes next ,
that *Something* follows *Come Together*,
how *Golden Slumbers* morphs into *Carry that Weight*,
the way I can sing the upcoming notes before they are played,
how I know almost every word from every track
by heart;
maybe someday they'll play one of their CDs
over and over,
one hundred times, two hundred times,
like we played that record in the fall of '69,
the early months of '70,
down in the church basement,
the one we converted into a coffee house
called the Free Spirit,
spent hours playing pool with that album on the phonograph,
finished Side One *I Want You*,
flipped it over *Here Comes the Sun*, again and again
so that now, in my car forty-five years later,
when the songs play
I hear the echoes of billiard balls
click and clack together —
a background accompaniment
of percussive apparitions.

II.
The studio and crosswalk are still here,
but the painted lines are different now,
the street bustling with traffic;
tourists wait patiently until it's clear
in both directions,
step out and walk to the opposite corner,
picturing the album cover —
first John in white suit and tennis shoes,
Ringo in black with boots,
Paul barefoot, cigarette in his right hand,
George last in denim blue.

We cross the street today
and despite all the years and changes,
there is a connection,
a contentment,
knowing we are here
where they were.

Symphony

Minutes after five,
early in the morning,
the performance began.
At first,
a single engine carried the melody,
mournful siren-flute,
soft at first,
persistent,
volume increasing.
Now, joined by another,
picking up the tune,
playing a rondo,
wailing a duet.
The sudden blast of a trumpet,
music growing louder,
a third voice is added,
rumble of the ladder truck,
sirens intertwining,
harmonizing,
notes repeating,
neo-classical fugue.

The melody softens,
diminished by distance.
And I hear for the first time
percussion —
staccato of the rain,
drumming,
carrying the beat,
continuing alone.

From the back

the stranger looks familiar
as he stands near the car,
gestures with his hands,
shoulders slightly hunched

as he stands near the car,
short, white hair cap-covered,
engrossed in conversation,

gestures with his hands,
wears a short-sleeved sweatshirt
despite February wind,

shoulders slightly hunched,
he could be my dad,
and I don't want him to turn around.

An Unfinished Book

It sounded intriguing:
the Human Library,
a safe place where people
become books,
where visitors are given
an opportunity to listen,
ask questions about taboo topics,

to "read" the living books.

And so he went to the event,
looked at the selections —
Alcoholic, Feminist,
Convert, Unemployed,
Naturist, Disabled —
decided, at last, on *Refugee,*
took a seat at her table.

In precise English,
softly accented,
she told her story,
where she once lived,
her escape from violence
and oppression,
where she lives now,
in this city filled with stares,
distrust, prejudice.

She was an open book,

honest, inspiring, strong,
authentic,
and they shared similar dreams,
hopes for the future.

He lingered
after the other readers had gone,
asked her to tell another chapter,
didn't want this book
to end.

Memory*

Once, in Oregon December, you *let*
notes fly from a silver trumpet, with *me*
watching from a window, wishing I could *teach*
the song to linger in the trees *like*
wind in the branches, like *the*
way love feels at the very *first*,
pure and nourishing like fresh *snow*,
like music rising and *falling*.

**A Golden Shovel poem… with thanks for
the final line of* Undivided Attention
by Taylor Mali.

Hybrid

In a vacant lot
near duplexes multi-generation crowded,
the immigrants are growing vegetables.
One block from the modern supermarket
they kneel and fill baskets,
wearing straw hats and skirts,
sandaled feet longing to immerse again
in muddy waters of rice fields.
Uprooted and transplanted from villages,
families dig and pull weeds,
maintaining traditions,
claiming this land
simply by working the soil —
dirt between toes,
under fingernails,
nurtured by earth.

Now, at autumn harvest,
election advertisements sprout up
along the planted boundaries;
cardboard placards rooted in political freedom,
staked alongside rows of native corn,
grafting cultures.

Savored Gifts

I.
Like gray rippled glass,
the Thames flows slowly past
the bench where I sit,
past Parliament houses
lit in soft gold at dusk
as the melody begins —
sixteen notes
followed by reverberating chimes
I feel within me,
deep and recognizable,
quintessential London.

II.
Surrounded by a drum corps hornline
arced into a huge half circle,
I stand in a stadium parking lot
as gloved hands
raise over seventy silvery
trumpets, mellophones, baritones
to begin their warm-up —
a series of musical scales in unison,
notes ascend, descend, devolve briefly
into cacophony —
blend together again,
begin to play the anthem
from a show years before,
my favorite of all time,
and I close my eyes
to savor this gift.

III.
In mixed shade and sun under pine trees,
I rest on a massive granite boulder
in Happy Isles,
the Merced River at season's fullness.
Icy water rushes over rocks, under bridges,
churns rapids into whiteness,
mists my face,
fills my ears with
continuous thunder

as spring roars into the Valley.

Interfaith Thanksgiving at Beth Shalom

When the imam stood on the bima
and began to chant from the Holy Quran,
there was a second of surprise,
like an imperceptible flicker
from the *ner tamid*
high on the wall behind him

and the synagogue members
may have held their breath
just for those few first notes
until the verses carried clearly,
echoing the Hebrew prayer chanted minutes before
by the Rabbi —
two languages so similar in sounds and cadence,
the Arabic words filled the sanctuary,
touched the prayer books in pews,
sang to the large menorah on the wall,
found their way, even,
to the Torah scrolls hidden in the Ark,
and surrounded all of us who sat
listening
at this celebration of
Thanks-giving,
imbued with a new understanding
of an old truth:
that sometimes it takes
just as much courage
and risk
to remind us less of our differences
than what we have in common.

Four Mile Trail in Spring

Switchbacks
zigzag steep granite cliffs,
a relentless incline
that takes our breath away,
like the view across the Valley to El Capitan,
Yosemite Falls in full spring splendor,
its roar a constant background
as we ascend the trail,
turn a corner,
continue to climb.

Lizards sun on rocks,
ravens call, soar,
perform acrobatics in the air
as we slowly gain elevation,
gaze westward toward the Central Valley,
eastward up Tenaya Canyon,
downward to the Merced River,
a snake of blue
curving and shimmering below us.

Finally,
at Glacier Point,
we sit on rocks,
share food, water, conversation,
look across at Vernal and Nevada Falls,
the majesty of Half Dome,
a panorama muted like a painted mural,
analgesic balm
for aching muscles
and our souls.

Tribute to Neva

I.
The tulips from your memorial service are open now,
the vase on the window sill,
yellow, orange, purple, dark red petals, translucent
like bone china,
lean on long-leafed stems, a gentle bend from the vase.
Outside in the back yard,
the mourning doves are nesting in our Boston fern,
bright goldfinches eat from the feeder
along with white-crowned sparrows,
like your collection of ceramic figurines,
the Lenox china blue bird, robins, dove,
golden crowned kinglet,
displayed on shelves in your apartment,
carefully positioned in the china cabinet,
and I picture the way you fed the birds in Sunriver,
mashed peanut butter into cream of wheat,
spread the mixture on the feeders, stood in the yard,
arms outstretched,
the chickadees landing on your hands,
your palms held upward,

the way you lived your life.

II.
Twice widowed,
you asked that your remains be placed in the earth
next to both husbands
in a cemetery miles away, rarely visited.
So we saved some ashes before the burial,
mixed them with a few of my father's,
scattered them in Oregon
at the base of trees and plants near your two homes,
under the large cross at the community church,
around a bench donated in memory of your closest friends,
into currents of the Deschutes River.

This is how we will remember you,
not buried on a Palos Verdes hillside,
but under pine trees and bitter brush,
among tiny purple blossoms in the groundcover
that blankets the berm —
a part of Sunriver
to be touched by birds, deer,
or the squirrels you loved,
at rest under clear blue skies
and at night,
a million stars.

9/11

At the gym, the wall of flatscreens in front of me,
I look up to see an image of smoke billowing into
blue September skies,
blackened tops of the Twin Towers,
the all-too-familiar news footage
we have now watched for the past eighteen years
but still can't look away from.
A woman tells her story of survival,
how a young man found her and others
in the 78th floor sky lobby,
guided them to the one remaining stairway,
led everyone down seventeen floors,
then turned around and headed back to help others
a second time, then a third.

My legs pump on the elliptical machine
as I imagine him climbing those steps,
again and again,
a red bandanna around his nose and mouth,
and now his parents are speaking,
talking about this first-born son, a volunteer firefighter,
who offered first aid to other victims,
helped put out fires on other floors,
then disappaeared forever when the tower collapsed.

I grab a towel to wipe my face,
unable to hold back the tears,
not so much for this twenty-four year old hero,
but because I know with certainty
that my son, at exactly the same age,
himself a medic and firefighter volunteer,
would have done the same thing.

And just for those few moments,
it's as though I lost him.

Reflections on Stained Glass

I.
Before he understood the language of Torah,
before he understood its lessons in translation,
he knew the shul,
knew the feel of the prayer book in his hands
each Shabbat morning,
the stained glass Star of David in the window
near their regular seat,
he and his grandfather,
and after the service was over,
after the Kiddush, the challah,
a small sip of wine,
they walked home together,
his grandfather telling stories
of the Great Synagogue in Warsaw
where he prayed as a child,
the steps below the towering columns in front,
the three large doors,
and, best of all,
a dome like a crown on top.
Many years later,
his grandfather told him the rest of the story,
how his beloved shul was destroyed
after he left Poland,
how it was obliterated after the ghetto uprising.

II.
Today, he visits the Nożyk Synagogue,
the only prewar Jewish house of prayer
left standing,
a miraculous survivor of the Warsaw ghetto,
used by the SS as a stables and depot.
He puts on a tallis,
walks down the center aisle,
admires the columns, deep-set windows,
arches and filigree designs on the women's balcony,
stands in a pew,
rocks back and forth
as he recites Kaddish for his grandfather,
for all those who once worshipped here,
remembers the Jewish legend
that promises the prayers of previous generations
will stick to the walls like dust,
forever binding them
to those of the present,
carrying them both
into the future.

How to Make Apricot Jam in Modesto

First of all,
you must wait until one of the hottest days in July,
a morning when the east window
is already too warm to touch
as you pull up the accordion shade,
when you can't imagine spending two hours
standing at the kitchen sink
while the dishwasher throbs and cleans the jars,
the metal lids and rings bubble and bang together
on the stove
as you hold the soft, velvet suede fruit
and gently cut each one in half,
the knife following a perfect indentation
formed there during growth,
the pit falling out cleanly
(not stubbornly reluctant like the nectarine),
then mashing, measuring sugar citric acid Vitamin C pectin
before placing the heavy pot on the stove
and starting to stir

and stir

and stir

and stir,

the steam rising into your face as you wait
for a rolling boil,
the golden mixture writhing wildly,
droplets jumping onto the stovetop,
until, at last, it's ready to ladle into sterile jars,
immerse in another boiling bath,
glass rattling against glass and metal lids
in hot steamy rhythm
that ends when the jars are removed,
turned upside down,
lined up on the counter to cool
while you clean the mess,
invert the jars,
wait for the tiny sucking sound as the jar exhales
to seal the lid

and dream of January morning biscuits.

The Antebellum Ladies' Nudist Society

I.
Twice a month
during those unbearably hot
humid weeks of summer,
they come together
on a day when house slaves are occupied with cleaning
and field slaves toil a mile away,
walk slowly as a group of three,
fan themselves, laughing, talking
until they reach the secluded spot,
the deep pool surrounded by trees,
where delicate white hands
untie hat ribbons,
remove lace gloves,
slip off dainty shoes,
unbutton dresses,
unlace stiff boned corsets,
pull off thin cotton undergarments
until they stand naked
and unashamed,
slip one by one into cool water,
freed at last
from all restraints.

II.
Every evening
after the children are asleep,
when their men lay snoring
from their day's labor in the fields,
the women put down their sewing,
blow out the candles,
sneak from the cabins,
brown bare feet silent on rough boards,
the packed dirt path down to the river
familiar in darkness.
They follow each other in silence
to the shallow banks,
pull the coarse, unbleached cotton dresses
over their heads,
step over smooth, polished rocks
until they reach the water,
wade in without hesitation,
dipping to immerse themselves
into their only feeling
of total freedom.

Jigsaw Puzzles

I.
An opened box reveals
a thousand tiny pieces.
I take handfuls,
spread them on the dining table,
separate them into groups:
faces of people,
bits of wheels, wagons and horses,
mountains and sky,
windows, doors, letters, words,
buildings, roofs.

The ones with straight edges
create a frame;
an empty rectangle,
it lures me back
again and again
from household chores,
entices me with its
incompleteness.

II.
When I was in elementary school,
my grandmother
shared her puzzles with me,
an old, rickety card table
set up in her small living room.

The one I remember most
was a seascape,
a shipwreck, perhaps,
with expanses of dark green, brown,
murky and difficult.
I would pick up piece after piece,
frustrated, ready to give up,
but she taught me to look for small details,
match shapes, colors, designs,
to be patient.

As we worked to create the image,
she talked to me about school,
friends, future plans —

the puzzle an excuse
to spend time together.

That Spring Feeling

Once in a while,
waiting to turn left at a traffic light,
the green arrow appears but nobody moves;
horns honk,
windows roll down
and then,
as if it were rehearsed,
drivers jump from their cars
run to the front of the line —
total strangers working as a team,
suddenly brought together,
pushing the conked-out car
through the intersection to safety.

Cynics will say their motive
is selfish,
that they simply want this impediment
out of the way
so they can rush on.
But there's something about that
spontaneous reaction
that makes me remember
unselfish goodness

and never fails to
restore my faith
in humanity.

Under the Milky Way

Kauai Memories

Waves thunder,
break for miles along the shore;
foam laces the sand,
pulls back, returns,
washes, recedes,
rhythmical breaths from the ocean,
pulse of the island.

Hens and roosters
forage in every park and parking lot,
along roadways, yards, sugar cane,
constant cluck and crow,
background music of the island.

Rain slickens
red dirt,
smooths into slippery clay
on Waimea Canyon
hiking trails,
paprika color of the island.

In Camp Curry

At night
as we walk back from the amphitheater,
the cabins glow like paper lanterns,
each one illuminated by one bare bulb
with shadowy shapes moving inside
cream-colored canvas,
voices clearly audible
through split seams, open flaps —
no protection against the acrid smell
of campfire smoke
or pre-dawn's chill
that seeps into all the corners
where warmth and privacy
are only illusions,
and all of us are like one family
sleeping in the same large room
under the Milky Way.

English Lake Country

On a steep edge
of Cat Bells fell,
I sit surrounded by
Cumbria's Lake District,
a Wordsworthian landscape
of sharp ridges easing to soft slopes,
darkened in places like worn velvet,
flattening to lush fields
bordered with Douglas fir, oak, spruce,
hues of hunter, forest, pine —
every variation from a one-color palette
stretching out beneath my feet;
sheep scamper up rocky paths
through fern-filled hillsides,
the sun warms my back,
reflects off smooth surface
of Derwent Water behind me,
in this living calendar picture
I imprint into my memory
to keep it always

evergreen.

To Half Dome

Until today I always maintained
a respectful distance.
Amid pantheistic splendor, I stood humbly
within the walls of this glacier-carved cathedral
worshipping you from afar.
I sat at your feet on a Mirror Lake sandbar,
paying homage.
Like the Indian maiden etched upon your face,
you were out of reach, forever inaccessible
until today
when I rose in darkness,
determined to climb granite stairways,
to climb the way of waterfalls,
to climb to a higher valley,
to climb for five hours to reach the final challenge,
feet finally touching your back — slick, steep —
gloved hands grasping cables,
pulling, pulling, as you waited in silent grandeur
for me to reach your summit,
to see the world from your perspective,
perceive your sovereignty
and stand, at last,
upon your shoulders.

Ancient Roads in Ireland

At Brú na Bóinne,
Neolithic ancestors walked on ancient roads
through sacred land
toward prehistoric passage graves
and ceremonial temples like Newgrange,
where grass grows atop a rounded mound,
over white quartz walls layered with earth and stone,
carved circles, spirals, chevrons, arcs;
created by a people older than the Pyramids and Stonehenge
who feared the loss of light in autumn's abbreviated days.

This holy place keeps a secret all year long
until dawn of Winter Solstice
when a rising sun peeks in through a roofbox
aligned to capture the rays,
sends them to the inner chamber,
flooding the floor with light –
an annual miracle providing reassurance
that the days,
once again,
will begin to lengthen.

I speak to the raven

at Olmstead Point
as he struts proudly
across the asphalt lot,
glossy and black
like winged obsidian.
I admonish him,
because he is too elegant
to walk between cars,
hop the curb to the overlook,
lower himself to the wiles
of a marmot or Steller's Jay,
become a common beggar.

He cocks his head to listen,
speaks in guttural clicks and knocks,
then gives a mournful,
hollow, high-pitched murmur
to admit his lapse of discretion,
lowers his body,
pushes forward off the ground,
spreads his wings and soars over the wall,
floats down into the Valley
with regal grace,
befitting a messenger of Odin.

BART Rides

I.
Two teenage boys board
at Oakland Coliseum station,
Raiders caps over dreadlocks,
torn jeans sagged well below the waist,
earplugs in, phones in hand,
a strong smell of marijuana
following them to the last two seats.

She enters with a crowd at Montgomery,
Louis Vuitton bag over one shoulder,
gray hair pulled back in a tight chignon,
Old Money tastefully exhibited,
hurriedly grabs the overhead strap
near the boys' seats,
balances herself as the train lurches forward.

At Powell Street, one of the boys gets up to leave,
his empty seat an unspoken invitation.
She hesitates, sits by the window,
turns her head to look out at the platform,
then stares into darkness all the way to Civic Center.

II.
After we board at Embarcadero Station,
the train plunges into downward darkness,
speeds through the tunnel under the bay.
Ears pop, a mild unease permeates the car,
and I wonder how many passengers
think about an earthquake at this moment —
a derailment, shattered windows, the rush of cold water —
or, like me, simply wonder,

How is it even possible to build a submerged railway
over three miles long under 135 feet of water?

When they were younger,
my granddaughters would ask to sit near the window,
hoping to see fish swim by
or maybe a whale;
this makes me smile as the train screams and wails,
wheels dragging against the rails on turns,
and then, suddenly, we climb up into daylight,
emerge like some kind of mechanical sea serpent.

III.
I stare out the window
at giant dock cranes like Imperial walkers from *Star Wars*,
multicolored graffiti murals on buildings and walls,
block-long fences topped with razor wire,
homeless camps under elevated ramps,
signs and billboards —
SUNSHINE BISCUITS,

JESUS IS ALIVE —
a burned-out home with a collapsed roof,
train cars stacked like giant blocks.
A pigeon perches on a station wall,
a seagull glides toward the Bay,
a jet floats on final approach to Oakland
with nose up, wheels down,
lush green hills on my left fringed with trees,
west-facing windows ablaze with the setting sun
as dusk falls
and we fly between two freeways.

An Event of Astronomical Proportions

One summer night
decades ago
a once-in-a-lifetime meteorite
streaked across the sky
over Yosemite Valley,
creating the illusion of daylight
that lasted for seconds,
lighting up the meadow
and towering rock walls before us
with celestial resplendence

More memorable
than the spectacle itself
was in that moment afterwards —
hundreds of voices shouted
and echoed around us,
tourists from across the globe,
witnesses to the same event,
all of us united
in one universal language
of amazement.

Titanic

Many of the wealthy men who traveled First Class
would have forgiven the captain and crew
for the excessive speed,
unheeded warnings,
their audacity and over-confidence.
It was, after all,
the way they conducted business —
earning the money that enabled them
to take their wives and servants
on a decadent pleasure cruise
for no other reason than simply
because they could.

But many of the other passengers,
the tinsmith, tailor and shoemaker,
the miner, mason,
baker and bricklayer
who perished in the freezing water,
led simple, slow,
careful lives,
saving money to purchase passage
on a regal ship,
wanting nothing more than a chance
to do better in America,
going aboard with families, belongings,
dreams of fulfillment

and clinging, in the end,
to buoyant hopes
and dreams
that remain ever
unsinkable.

The Deer

With reckless confidence
the deer leapt
gracefully,
proudly,
wildly
from the forest
onto Highway 140,
running directly in front of the car ahead of us

without screams or squealing brakes,
just a silent scene
that somehow overpowered the roar
of spring's waterfalls
for the rest of that day —
a vision of death
that flickered into focus
over and over,
even as we stood in boggy meadows,
gazed at granite splendor surrounding us,
feeling like guilty trespassers

in a place
that can never be both safe
and wild.

Mariposa Reenactment

I.
I sometimes wake before Reveille,
canvas tent cold and damp,
my breath in clouds,
the clang of cast iron pots as fires are kindled,
quiet voices of breakfast preparation.
I untie and open the flap,
step outside into a dark blue world,
streaks of light on the eastern horizon,
soldiers sitting together on logs
as I walk toward the warmth,
grab a towel to lift the enamelware pot,
pour boiling water into my mug,
sip tea as wild turkeys call to one another,
horses neigh,
dawn breaks.

II.
At night,
we walk up the hill to look at the stars,
gaze down on the camps,
triangles of tents,
the glow of lanterns and fires,
a return to a simpler time
without TV and cell phones,
like being in a time machine
transported to another century.

Flight QZ8501

Perhaps the jet left a vapor trail
signature in the sky,
filled with content passengers,
talking, reading, sleeping,
nothing to see below but water
on the flight to Singapore,
until the advent of the storm,
deceitful spurious clouds
with evil strength to become
the Arbiter of Life and Death,
clouds that grew icy tentacles,
grabbed the airliner and tossed it,
turned it into a graceless swan,
falling headfirst
into an unforgiving ocean.

To Vernal Falls

This trail is a siren.
She calls to us in our tent cabin,
lures us to Happy Isles again and again;
a temptress,
she knows we can't resist the challenge,
knows the effort is too addictive.

This trail is a trickster.
Her smooth, hard-packed façade feels deceptively easy
at first;
she hides her steep climbs,
waits until we've gone too far to turn back,
then rises sharply,
dares us to keep going, taunts us as our hearts pound,
our lungs fill with thin mountain air.

This trail is an old friend.
Our feet know her bends and curves,
ascents and descents,
rough-hewn granite steps,
where to stop and catch our breath,
where to stop to catch a glimpse
of Yosemite Falls, Illilouette,
where to sit against the granite wall,
where to stand on the wooden bridge.

This trail is a benefactress.
She refreshes us with a fine, delicate mist
on slick, steep cliffs,
serenades us with roar of whitewater churning,
tumbling over boulders,
falling behind a rainbow
in sparkling white thunder.

Road Trip, 1958

I spent hours that first day
looking at desert landscape,
cacti, sagebrush and distant mountains
that never seemed to change.
At some point my father said we were leaving Arizona,
entering New Mexico, and I looked up expectantly,
ready to see a long black line, a clear-cut division
between the states like my grade-school maps;
instead, I saw a sign, "Leaving Arizona"
followed immediately by a second sign,
"Welcome to New Mexico."
Just that.
No other demarcation,
nothing to show this state ended, the next state began,
no change in the scenery along Route 66,
simply an invisible border
between this mesquite tree and the one four feet away,
a pattern repeated daily as we headed east
into Texas, Oklahoma, Missouri,

as I gradually came to realize that this country
wasn't multi-colored states drawn into rectangles,
squares, or odd shapes whose sides
fit perfectly in a jigsaw puzzle;
the land transformed naturally,
dissolving from desert into fields of corn and beans,
to mountains and cities,
where margins and boundaries
didn't exist except on paper,
or perhaps in the minds of the surveyors,
ranchers and farmers
who walked the ground every day —
the land unchanged
for hundreds,
even thousands, of years.

Borderless
stretching forever.

Evening in Dresden

Buskers perform
with violin and guitar,
amplified "Allelujah" fills the city square,
rises over steep red roofs and gables,
encircles raindrops that fall on wet polished stones,
drifts off toward the Elbe River.

Behind us,
a horse-drawn carriage enters the plaza,
hooves echo on the uneven cobbled street,
and now,
as though rehearsed and timed perfectly,
church bells begin to toll the hour,
their loud sonorous peals
ascending to halo the heads of golden angels atop spires,
proclaiming joy and triumph
for this once bombed-out city,
this German phoenix
risen from the ashes of war.

No Fear of Flying

In that moment just before boarding,
I raise my hand to touch you with *Namaste,*
a ritual greeting of skin on metal,
a connection of human and machine
that affirms my trust,
acknowledges your power;
your heart beats beneath my feet,
your voice whines with excitement
as we are pushed from the gate,
your arms dip somewhat clumsily,
awkward, like a plump goose,
for this is not your element,
not your comfort zone,
you are destined for greater things,
impatient,
as you wait now at the end of the runway,
I sense your restless spirit,
feel you straining to break free,
a thoroughbred held back, reined in
until you are let loose,
and there's a pause as you catch your breath,
begin to lope, then sprint,
and a smile forms below your nose
as you start to roar,
raise your head and lift your feet —
for this is what you were made to do,
this is what you do best,
this is your domain, yours alone,
where you carry me with utter confidence,
and I am no longer afraid.

Photo at Dewey Point

My critical eye fixates immediately
on signs of the seventy-first birthday
I recently celebrated:
my head crowned in white,
a bustline that droops,
crepe-paper arms and knobby knees,
veins visible in my legs.

My grateful eye looks past these petty concerns:
El Capitan behind me,
the panoramic view to Yosemite's high country,
notes the Fitbit on my left arm
that will later confirm I hiked
eleven-plus miles on this six-hour trek
through meadows filled with wildflowers,
between pine trees, over granite boulders,
accompanied by chatter and laughter
of teenage grandchildren
as we made up limericks and puns
using names of Civil War generals,
listened to the calls of ravens,
watched them hop from cliffs to soar
on invisible currents of air,
glide back to perch on branches of ponderosa.

My heart sees what my eyes missed at first glance:
the beauty of this place,
the strength I still have,
and, as he has done now for over fifty years —
the man who stands next to me.

If I Had to Write a Poem about the Moon

Recently, I heard someone say
that every poet must have at least one poem about the moon,
and if that's true,
surely there can't be many new thoughts to add
to the thousands of words already written,
to the clichés about cheese, werewolves, lunatics, lovers,
tides, gravity, a Cheshire cat's smile.
Since my poetic legitimacy is apparently at stake,
I suppose I could write about the time
I hiked to Half Dome one October,
sunset coming early,
catching us above Nevada Falls,
our flashlights feeble in utter darkness
until a full moon rose over granite walls
like some kind of spiritual presence,
cast silver light on the trail
as we slowly made our way down to Happy Isles,
grateful for this celestial luminescence…
or I could divulge a secret about
the small window we added
to our second-story shower stall,
my favorite place to stand in darkness
naked and unseen
while cool water splashes on tile,
and I watch the moon as it glows
over this Central Valley,
waxing and waning,
sometimes disappearing,
other times full and round
like tonight
in almost-summer.

Journey

Her fortune read,
"You will travel to many exotic places,"
so she left the restaurant,
got into her car
and drove until she was sleepy,
stopping at the Motel 6 in Redding
which wasn't very exotic,
but it wasn't home

and when she stopped the next day
in Bend, Oregon,
she opted for lunch at
a Chinese buffet where her fortune,
this time, told her,
"Every exit is an entrance to new experiences,"
so she left via the emergency door,
ignoring the clanging alarm
and drove over the pass
to Springfield,
then on to Eugene,
stopping at an Asian market
where she bought an entire bag
of fortune cookies,
opened them all, one by one,
sitting on the queen bed
in her motel room
until she found just the one
she wanted,
leaving the next morning
heading south,
going home.

About the Author

An educator for over three decades, Nancy Haskett retired in 2011 and is a member of the Ina Coolbrith Circle and Modesto-Stanislaus Poetry Center, as well as her local writing group, the Sestina Sisters. She has presented her poetry at the Carnegie Arts Center in Turlock, in Modesto's city council chambers, and at the long-running Barkin' Dog "Second Tuesday" showcase, among other venues. Her work has appeared in more than forty publications and on-line forums, both regional and national. In her free time, Nancy enjoys reading, traveling, hiking among nature's wonders, and spending time with her family. She and her husband Mark live in Modesto, California.

Grateful acknowledgement is made to the following publications where these poems or previous versions of them have appeared:

Baseball Bard: *When I was nine*

Blackwidow's Web of Poetry: *Crime Scene; Wagon Train Girlhood*

California Poets website: *The Antebellum Ladies' Nudist Society*

The Cannon's Mouth: *A New Beginning*

A Circle of Voices: *Baltimore: April 29, 2015; Mariposa Reenactment; Upward Climb*

The Gathering 13: *Abbey Road*

The Gathering 15 Anthology: *Upward Climb*

Gatherings 12: *Roller Skates*

Hildegard Festival: *Shadows and Reflections; Wagon Train Girlhood*

Homestead Review: *Abbey Road; Crayola Memories; Flight QZ8501; Road Trip, 1958*

Little Eagle Press Re/Verse: *Shadows and Reflections*

Long Story Short e-zine: *Make Believe; Shadows and Reflections; Sometimes I mourn the loss of fog; Wagon Train Girlhood*

Loon Magic and Other Night Sounds: *Symphony*

Lucky Jefferson 365 Collection: *Journey*

manymore: *That Spring Feeling*

Medusa's Kitchen: *Abbey Road; At Grandma Becky's; Baltimore: April 29, 2015; The Antebellum Ladies' Nudist Society; Berkeley, 1969; Confession to Anne Frank; Crime Scene; Eulogy; Fabrication; Final Evaluation; The immigrant in 1900; I speak to the raven; Metaphor; The Missing Piece; Native; No Fear of Flying; Obituary; On "Landscape with the Fall of Icarus"; Subdivision; Upward Climb; Wagon Train Girlhood; Watching A Hard Day's Night Fifty Years Later; William; What has happened*

Miller's Pond Poetry Journal: *Confession to Anne Frank; Native; On "Landscape with the Fall of Icarus"*

Mistlin Art Gallery: *Reflections on Stained Glass (Collision V exhibit); Upward Climb (Collision V exhibit)*

Monterey Poetry Review: *Change Gonna Come; Metaphor; Requiem for Scott*

The Moon: *If I Had to Write a Poem about the Moon*

More than Soil, More than Sky: *Roller Skates; William*

National League of American Penwomen website: *Ancient Roads in Ireland; Awaiting the Tooth Fairy; Hurricane Dogs; If I Had to Write a Poem about the Moon; Interfaith Thanksgiving; Make Believe; A New Beginning; Native; November, 1963; When I was nine; Sometimes I mourn the loss of fog; Sunriver; Tribute to Neva*

New Year's Poetry Challenge chapbook: *Memory*

Our Cup of Tea: *Journey*

The Pen: *In Camp Curry*

Penwoman Magazine: *Handed Down; English Lake Country; If I Had to Write a Poem about the Moon; Memory; Wagon Train Girlhood; War Is Not Healthy for Children*

The Poeming Pigeon: *Abbey Road*

Poems of the Super Moon: *If I Had to Write a Poem about the Moon*

Poets' Corner: *At the Edge; Berkeley, 1969; Crayola Memories; Crime Scene; Crows; The Deer; Eulogy; Final Evaluation; How to Make Apricot Jam in Modesto; Hybrid; In Camp Curry; Interfaith Thanksgiving at Beth Shalom; Internment; The Missing Piece; Protest; Ride 'Em Cowgirl; Roller Skates; Scented Nostalgia; Science Lesson; Subdivision; Sunriver; Symphony; Titanic; To Half Dome; The Truth about Santa; When I was nine*

Poets of the San Joaquin Anthology: *William*

Penumbra Journal: *BART Rides; Notre Dame; Shadows and Reflections*

Song of the San Joaquin: *After the Pandemic; At Grandma Becky's; Classic Blue; Crime Scene; Crows; Dentists; Doppelganger; Dust; Gardenias; Handed Down; Hybrid; If I Had to Write a Poem about the Moon; I speak to the raven; Just Desserts; Liquid Alchemy; Mariposa Reenactment; My son knows death; Orphans; Photo at Dewey Point; Sometimes I mourn the loss of fog; Subdivision; That Spring Feeling; To the Young Man Whose Invitation I Declined; Tribute to Neva; What has happened; When I was nine; 1967; 9/11*

Stanislaus Connections: *Berkeley, 1969; Crows; Fabrication; On "Landscape with the Fall of Icarus"; Protest; Shadows and Reflections; Subdivision; War Is Not Healthy for Children*

Updrafts: *Obituary*

Weekly Avocet: *At the Edge; That Spring Feeling*

The following poems were winners of awards in various poetry contests, both local and national:

An Event of Astronomical Proportions / California Federation of Chaparral Poets, 2013

A New Beginning / Ina Coolbrith Circle, 2019

An Ode to Ice Cream / California Federation of Chaparral Poets, 2021

At Grandma Becky's / Jeannette Gould Maino, 2003 / Voices of Lincoln, 2016

At the Edge / California Federation of Chaparral Poets, 2014

Awaiting the Tooth Fairy / Modesto-Stanislaus Poetry Center annual festival, 2018

Baltimore: April 29, 2015 / Ina Coolbrith Circle, November, 2015 / Roseville Friends of the Library, 2015 / Modesto-Stanislaus Poetry Center annual festival, 2016 / National League of American Penwomen, Biennial Letters category, 2016

BART Rides / Ina Coolbrith Circle contest, 2017 / Modesto-Stanislaus Poetry Center annual festival contest, 2018

Boots / Jeannette Gould Maino contest, 2006

Crayola Memories (*previously titled A Box of Crayons*) / Modesto-Stanislaus Poetry Center annual festival, 2015 / National League of American Penwomen, Biennial Letters category, 2016

Crime Scene / Voices of Lincoln, 2011

Crows / Jeannette Gould Maino, 2003

Dear NPR / Ina Coolbrith Circle, 2019

Fabrication / Modesto-Stanislaus Poetry Center annual festival, 2020

Fifty years later / California Federation of Chaparral Poets, 2021

Hurricane Dogs / Jeannette Gould Maino, 2006 / Voices of Lincoln, 2011

The immigrant in 1900 / Ina Coolbrith Circle, 2015 & 2017 / Roseville Friends of the Library, 2016 / Voices of Lincoln, 2017

Internment / California Federation of Chaparral Poets, 2013

Made By Hand / Jeannette Gould Maino, 2007

Memory / California Federation of Chaparral Poets, 2020

Notre Dame / Modesto-Stanislaus Poetry Center annual festival, 2020

Obituary / Jeannette Gould Maino, 2005 / California Federation of Chaparral Poets, 2013

Please Don't Hold a Carwash for My Funeral / Ina Coolbrith Circle, 2013 / Voices of Lincoln, 2014

Protest / California Federation of Chaparral Poets, 2012

The Rat in the Bird Feeder / Ina Coolbrith Circle, 2016

The Remains / California Federation of Chaparral Poets, 2014 / Modesto-Stanislaus Poetry Center annual festival, 2019

Reprimand / California Federation of Chaparral Poets, 2020

Roller Skates / Voices of Lincoln, 2017

Science Lesson / California Federation of Chaparral Poets, 2012

Shadows and Reflections / Modesto-Stanislaus Poetry Center annual festival, 2014 / National League of American Penwomen, Biennial Letters category, 2014

To the Young Man Whose Invitation I Declined / Ina Coolbrith Circle, 2017

Tribute to Neva / Ina Coolbrith Circle contest, 2018 / National League of American Penwomen, Biennial Letters category, 2022

Upward Climb / National League of American Penwomen, Biennial Letters category, 2020

Wagon Train Girlhood / Jeannette Gould Maino, 2005

When I was nine / NLAPW Nor-Cal writing contest, 2013

William / Jeannette Gould Maino, 2004

1967 / City of Benicia Love Poetry contest, 2021

3602 Petaluma Avenue / California Federation of Chaparral Poets, 2021